Insights Today

My

Journey With God

Davronia "Val" Scarbrough

Insights Today My Journey With God

Copyright © 2017 by Davronia "Val" Scarbrough

All rights reserved. Except as permitted under the U.S. Copyright Act of 1976, no part of this publication. No part of this book may be reproduced or transmitted in any form or by any means, electronic or mechanical, including photocopying, recording, or by any information storage and retrieval system, without permission in writing from the copyright owner.

ISBN: 978-0-9995498-0-3

Published November 2017

ScarbroughED Publisher

PO Box 25848

Charlotte, NC 28229

Introduction

This book would not be in existence if Holy Spirit had not spent time with me and orchestrated my thoughts to align with heavens views of earthly matters. So, before I go any further I want to say, "Thank You Sir"!

The sayings in this journal are things that have structured my life in good times and helped me to navigate through troublesome times. Living in this culture as a believer should help us even the more to see the real value of a life in Christ Jesus. This book derived from my observation of people in the work place, grocery stores, churches, and the general public. Meaningless opinions and values have wrapped around the minds and lives of people's social views, and morals; therefore, placing many Christians in a place of living their lives through carnality and refusing to take a stand for what is right (not to mention the word of God). With such a lax stance in our society, it has caused many to reduce their principles to encompass anything, simply to avoid living in the outskirts of acceptance.

Power over each other has become the "idol god" of today. For many people stress is the bed partner of an overwhelming majority. We focus on getting the status, but we lose our joy in the process. We focus on becoming prosperous at the cost of having no peace of mind. Life is worth living, humans shouldn't be willing to die in the futile pursuit of power.

My journey with God is to serve man-kind with inspiration for living and not just living any life, but one with purpose. Life should not be just a commodity, but a treasure we behold inside our earthen vessel. It is sad to see a man only start to value this wonderful life when he is faced with the last few minutes of it.

The word of God helps us "not" to put a price tag on who we are today, but for us to view our lives as priceless gems in eternity.

We are greater than mere diamonds, sapphires, rubies, pearls, and all the precious gems that have ever been created. We are God's greatest masterpieces.

Every sequence in our lives represents where we have been, where we are going, or where we are now. This book is designed to help us think about the places, things, and areas of our lives we want to work on or enhance to make us a greater witness for the kingdom of God.

Sometimes it just takes us looking at things for what they really are, being truthful about our state in life just like the woman at the well was challenged to do. The believer has the responsibility to take the necessary steps to change what we can (Ephesian 4:23) which is being renewed in the spirit of our minds.

God did not design this life of ours to be complicated, but he designed it to be a journey of seeking out Godly wisdom and applying the wisdom that he so freely shares with us, when we ask. The bible tells us in Proverbs 8 that Wisdom was there at the right hand of God when all things were created. So, then if wisdom was there at the creation, then wisdom should be with the "creation(wo/man)" as we travel this road called life.

Life is precious and a beauty to behold, but there is an end to this life on earth and how we approach it will make the difference in our eternity. As you read this book and take time to journal your thoughts "do not" just do it as something to past time, but make this journal apart of your time.

King Solomon said, "Life is but a vapor"; therefore, make each vaporizing moment count for something; because at the end of the day every word, action, thought, and behavior must be accounted for (Revelation 20:11-12) (Romans 14:10).

Enjoy Your Time with Our Jesus!

Val S.

Reading Instructions

This book has been designed to help in your daily walk with our Lord Jesus Christ and to embrace the wisdom of our father. Sometimes we need a place to put our personal thoughts. My hope and prayer are that you use this time to hear what the spirit is saying to the church(you). As Holy Spirit speaks to you, I pray the spirit of truth leads you to powerful transformation that will not be erased by the enemy.

You will find this book is set up for you to journal your own thoughts.

Note: NOT ALL of the quotations will have a following read to accompany the quote. Some quotations are for you to interpret as the reader. This journal has been designed to influence the reader to think past your current thought pattern and take on the mind of Christ. As believers, we should embrace a heavenly prospective on our everyday situations.

ENJOY!

These are basic characteristics of man(wo). When you can deal with the truth of who you are it makes facing yourself so much easier. Knowing who you are at the core; the good, the bad, the ugly helps one "to thyself be true". The words found below characterize the view many people have of themselves and some are descriptions that people don't want to face about themselves. Honesty can be difficult. My objective for placing these descriptions here along with their definitions is so the reader can have a personal mirror and use this time of journaling to look introspectively.

- ✓ **Self-Centered** - limited to or caring only about you and your own needs.
- ✓ **Unworthy** - lacking in value or merit
- ✓ **Trustworthy** - taking responsibility for one's conduct
- ✓ **Lonely** - marked by grief from being without help; addicted to solitude or seclusion from company.
- ✓ **Pureness** - being undiluted or unmixed with extraneous (not pertinent) material.
- ✓ **Truth** - the real facts about something (certainty/reality)
- ✓ **Overbearing** - expecting unquestioning obedience; too confident and too determined to tell other people what to do, in a way that is unpleasant and not easy to like; Aggressively haughty; arrogant; domineering; tyrannical; dictatorial; insolent.

- ✓ **Faith** – firm belief and trust in God. Firm belief in something for which you have yet to see the proof. Something that is believed in with strong conviction without question.

- ✓ **Love** – strong affection for another arising out of kinship or personal ties attraction based on sexual desire: affection and tenderness felt affection based on admiration, benevolence, or common interests
- ✓ **Unforgiveness** – unwilling or unable to forgive having or making no allowance for error or weakness

Definitions are from Merriam-Webster dictionary.

> *Life is simple; yet it has plenty of complexities wrapped around it; however, all of us must deal with the basics.*

In referenced to your former manner of life, you lay aside the old self, which is being corrupted in accordance with the lusts of deceit, and that you be renewed in the spirit of your mind

Ephesians 4:23

Truth is not what is perceived, but what is conceived

1. Perceive- to regard as being such: to become aware of through senses.
2. Conceive – to become pregnant with; to cause to begin; originate

The bible tells us we should be renewed in the spirit of our minds. The nature of man is to stamp truth around what he perceives, through his own experiences (what he sees), or misnomers (insecurities), or opinions (how he feels). These things fall under the category of **perception,** but the word of God falls under the category of **truth (**fidelity to an **original** or to a standard). So, my advice would be, **conceive** the word and allow it to grow in you and become a part of who you are, and leave perception alone.

Daily Read: Proverbs 14

My Thoughts:

_____
_____
_____

My Goal Today To Apply This Word

_____
_____
_____

How did I apply this word today?

_____
_____
_____

Self-Evaluation: Did I miss an opportunity to apply this wisdom today?

Don't run from it; Learn from it!

In my life travels, I have been fortunate enough to be included in the processing of many married couples. Many times, in the process, I see a common thread which is; couples would rather run from each other instead of learning from each other. When a mistake is made, FORGIVE. When words are said out of anger, REPENT. When you are misunderstood, be ACCOUNTABLE. When you have wronged another person, APOLOGIZE. Remember, let no man put asunder, not even you.

Now the great thing about this statement is, it's not just for married couples but for the masses. Remember, running is for those who have no desire to "change". Don't run from it; Learn from it!

Daily Read: Matthew 19

My Thoughts:

_____
_____
_____

My Goal Today to Apply This Word:

_____
_____
_____

How did I apply this word today?

_____
_____
_____

Self-Evaluation: Did I miss an opportunity to apply this wisdom today?

Limit your world; limit your potential

What if man had said putting letters together would never form sounds and words? Then there would be no language, dictionary, thesaurus, or an encyclopedia. What if man would have limited his views to the horse and buggy? Then there would be no automobiles. What if airplanes were never invented? Then there wouldn't be airports. When a man limits his world, he limits his potential to make a difference in the world in which he lives. Open your mind and you open your potential!

Daily Read: Matthew 17

My Thoughts:

_____
_____
_____

My Goal Today to Apply This Word:

_____
_____
_____

How did I apply this word today?

_____
_____
_____

Self-Evaluation: Did I miss an opportunity to apply this wisdom today?

Don't just dress for success; clothe yourself for your purpose

I believe purpose doesn't just happen, but purpose is a culmination of events in your life that prunes you for your destiny. Every job, every volunteering event you attend, every relationship you encounter directly or indirectly are clothing you for purpose. Remember the word of God tells us that "a righteous man's steps are ordered". So, if God orders our steps, and He is the one that has designed our purpose; don't you think He knows the classes needed to secure your success? So, from this day forward don't just dress for success, but clothe yourself with every event in your life. They are there for your PURPOSE!

Daily Read: Psalms 37

My Thoughts:

_____

_____

_____

My Goal Today to Apply This Word:

_____

_____

_____

How did I apply this word today?

_____

_____

_____

Self-Evaluation: Did I miss an opportunity to apply this wisdom today?

Peace comes when the passion to pursue your PURPOSE overrides and defies the critics

Peace is that place where you are most comfortable, and you are in what I call the "The Groove". Without a shadow of a doubt you know you were "born to do this". All of us were created to do something that is unique to our engineered existence. Often, more times than I care to acknowledge, people live their lives without tapping into the real reason for their existence. When we don't know the true purpose of our existence (the very reason we occupy our space here in the earth), we tend to lack true peace in our lives. When you tap into the peace of who you were created to be, your uniqueness, and your worth, "passion" kicks in and with every fiber of your being you go after your "PURPOSE" without reservation. Today I encourage you (if you haven't already) take time to find out why you were put here on the earth. Take the time to quiet your life down to earnestly pray and hear clearly what your purpose is, and then conquer any fear that tries to overtake your thoughts, or actions to live your life on Purpose!

Daily Read: Proverbs 4

My Thoughts:

_____

_____

_____

My Goal Today to Apply This Word:

_____

_____

_____

How did I apply this word today?

_____

_____

_____

Self-Evaluation: Did I miss an opportunity to apply this wisdom today?

Make your "Thought Life" count for something

Don't allow idle thoughts to invade your mind. When idleness invades our minds, it stunts our capacity for greatness. Challenge yourself to learn more, read more, memorize more, and dream more. A life of idleness is a slap in the face of the master craftsman, our Father. You were made for purpose and idleness suffocates purpose.

Daily Read: Proverbs 31:26-28 & Proverbs 14:22-24

My Thoughts:

_____
_____
_____

My Goal Today to Apply This Word:

_____
_____
_____

How did I apply this word today?

_____
_____
_____

Self-Evaluation: Did I miss an opportunity to apply this wisdom today?

Justifying who you are, "Limits" who you can become...

One day I was preparing for our women's meeting and Holy Spirit said to me talk to the ladies about the "measuring stick syndrome". I meditated on the statement and these thoughts were born. Most women carry a few things with them always. We carry a purse, a photo id, some type of lip moisturizer, an ink pen, and the <u>good old faithful "measuring stick"</u>. People are always measuring themselves against someone else and we always tend to come up short. Why? I believe people must have a sense of justification of who they are, where they are, and why they are there. I am no exception to that syndrome, but the thing I have come to realize is when we do that, we limit who we have the possibility of developing into. My worth was determined before I was a thought in my mothers' womb, or a seed assigned to my fathers' loins, and my purpose was set forth before the foundations of the earth. So, I ask you, why justify a masterpiece? Declare today, "You are a great you"!

Daily Read: Jeremiah 1:5

My Thoughts:

_____

_____

_____

My Goal Today to Apply This Word:

_____

_____

_____

How did I apply this word today?

_____

_____

_____

Self-Evaluation: Did I miss an opportunity to apply this wisdom today?

A person with limited "Views" is a person only concerned with their own opinions

Have you ever met someone, and their views seem to be the only right views, or their experiences seem to be the only valid experience? This is a person that has no concern for others and does not value what someone else can bring to their life. I have found this kind of person lives only according to their perspective, ideologies and only their concerns. The sad conclusion is; I would imagine it must be very lonely in that person's world. So, when you meet a person with those characteristics, pray for them to open their hearts to others as God has put us here for one another. Take time and learn a lesson from someone else today!

Daily Read: 1 Samuel 25

My Thoughts:

_____

_____

_____

My Goal Today to Apply This Word:

_____

_____

_____

How did I apply this word today?

_____

_____

_____

Self-Evaluation: Did I miss an opportunity to apply this wisdom today?

_____
_____
_____
_____
_____
_____
_____
_____
_____
_____
_____
_____
_____
_____
_____
_____
_____
_____
_____
_____

Count a man's "Views" worthless and you've purchased his self-esteem

Never allow what someone thinks of you to become what you think of yourself. Remember to "Cast Not Away YOUR Confidence, That Has Great Recompense "repay or payment" of REWARD". Your confidence has a payday.

Daily Read: Hebrew 10:35

My Thoughts:
_____
_____
_____

My Goal Today to Apply This Word
_____
_____
_____

How did I apply this word today?
_____
_____
_____

Self-Evaluation: Did I miss an opportunity to apply this wisdom today?

_____
_____
_____
_____
_____
_____
_____
_____
_____
_____
_____
_____
_____
_____
_____
_____
_____
_____
_____
_____
_____
_____

A person that finds his "Self-Worth" on the back of another person; is on an ego trip!

One of the biggest misnomers in one's life is the belief that your worth is substantiated through the eyes of someone else. When the bottom-line is, your worth is in who God has designed you to be! The truth is you are quite amazing!

#celebrateYourself

Daily Read: Luke 16

My Thoughts:
_____
_____
_____

My Goal Today to Apply This Word:
_____
_____
_____

How did I apply this word today?
_____
_____
_____

Self-Evaluation: Did I miss an opportunity to apply this wisdom today?

Recipe for Healthy Relationships: 1-cup of Confronting situations head-on, 1-cup of dispelling of lies, 1-cup of love, 1-cup of accountability, a pinch of tenderness, and 1-cup of mercy. Preheat your heart with forgiveness. Grease your mouth with truth. Stir all ingredients until they are well blended and bake whenever needed.

Daily Read: Proverbs 10

My Thoughts:

_____
_____
_____

My Goal Today to Apply This Word:

_____
_____
_____

How did I apply this word today?

_____
_____
_____

Self-Evaluation: Did I miss an opportunity to apply this wisdom today?

If you want to see the true nature of a man, give him POWER

In corporate America, there are always opportunities to see all types of people. For instance, there are "over-bearing" individuals (pushing their way to the top without a thought or regard for anyone). The "passive person", the "talkative person", the "quiet person", the "passive-aggressive" person, the "slow-learners", the "over-achiever", the "under-achiever", the "strictly 9-5" people (you can count on them not staying past 5:01). Then there are those who work for a company simply because they need a job; a better opportunity presents its self and they are out the door. These are all labels for "characteristics". However, there is a commonality they all have, and it is this, give them POWER and who they really are at the core of their being will be seen. I believe there are only four-groups of people: **The Pure, the Apathetic, the Greedy & the Malicious** these four "personalities" shape our society.

So, give a man(wo)man power and who they really are will be seen.

Daily Read: I Kings 11 & I Kings 12

My Thoughts:

_____

_____

_____

My Goal Today to Apply This Word:

_____

_____

_____

How did I apply this word today?

_____

_____

_____

Self-Evaluation: Did I miss an opportunity to apply this wisdom today?

Don't spend "PRICELESS" time with casual thinkers

This truth comes from watching Christian television one night. The Holy Spirit spoke to me and said, "casual thinkers are people who don't or can't conceive or respect the wisdom of God operating in another human vessel".

Jesus experienced casual thinkers throughout his ministry. Casual thinkers depend on their knowledge and declare it far outweighs the truth in God's word. They will never take the time to apply Godly principles to their natural circumstances. *1 Corinthians 1:27 states "But God has chosen the foolish things of the world to confound the wise.* So, for you to invest "Priceless" moments (something you will never get back) imparting into someone that will not allow the wisdom of God to flourish in their lives, you are wasting precious time and energy. Yes, always be concerned with a man's eternal destination, but don't spin your wheels with casual thinkers.

Daily Read: Luke 7:36-50

My Thoughts:

_____

_____

_____

My Goal Today to Apply This Word:

_____

_____

_____

How did I apply this word today?

_____

_____

_____

Self-Evaluation: Did I miss an opportunity to apply this wisdom today?

One of the biggest mistakes made by a person is when they allow arrogance to "Navigate" their lives!

Arrogance is the biggest deception known to man. When someone thinks their way of thinking, doing, and knowing is the only way to exist; that person becomes subject to living a life full of misguided direction. Many people could have avoided simple mistakes by opening their mind and life to the knowledge of someone else's wisdom. God placed us here for each other, and the greatest life to live is when we take advantage of the knowledge God gave to someone else just for us.

Daily Read: 2 Chronicles 32:25-27

My Thoughts:

_____

_____

_____

My Goal Today to Apply This Word:

_____

_____

_____

How did I apply this word today?

_____

_____

_____

Self-Evaluation: Did I miss an opportunity to apply this wisdom today?

_____
_____
_____
_____
_____
_____
_____
_____
_____
_____
_____
_____
_____
_____
_____
_____
_____
_____
_____
_____

You "cannot" help someone who does not feel you are qualified

A part of being made in the image of God is our empowerment to help others with emotional crisis. However, we also must take on the attitude of our father and not force our opinions or views on those who don't count them worthy of their attention. Over the years, I have found many people will want you to give them your time but not the wisdom of God you count invaluable. I had to come to the realization everyone that comes to me during a crisis doesn't necessarily count me worthy to speak into their lives. I learned very early in ministry not to take it personal and to be okay with others views of my qualifications.

Daily Read: Mark 6:1-6

My Thoughts:

_____
_____
_____

My Goal Today to Apply This Word:

_____
_____
_____

How did I apply this word today?

_____
_____
_____

Self-Evaluation: Did I miss an opportunity to apply this wisdom today?

***Pride**—* *unreasonable and inordinate self-esteem (personified as one of the deadly sins); a feeling of self-respect and personal worth.*

Don't internalize external words

You know today the world is full of people that internalize every word spoken to them and about them; which has caused us to live in a world of constant "OFFENSE". Why do we take to heart idle words spoken over and into our lives and yet disregard the words of God? My suggestion would be to get off-the-FENCE it's not that serious. If you live on the fence to long, you are bound to become raw. Remember the word of God is waiting to shape your world, so don't waste time internalizing empty words.

Daily Read: Acts 24:15-17

My Thoughts:

_____

_____

_____

My Goal Today to Apply This Word:

_____

_____

_____

How did I apply this word today?

_____

_____

_____

Self-Evaluation: Did I miss an opportunity to apply this wisdom today?

Lonely people, gossip about other people

Do you know someone that at the drop of a hat can just drive another person's character into the ground without a second thought? In my life's journey, I have run into so many people with this ability. So, one day I really started to think about that (because I use to live in the village called gossip as well). I stopped and said why am I talking about a person I don't know? I heard the Holy Spirit say, "You are lonely and haven't tapped into your purpose, because the moment you know what you were designed for, you will become so engrossed in that, your time will be too limited to speak on another person's life".

Daily Read: 1Timothy 5:13

My Thoughts:

_____
_____
_____

My Goal Today to Apply This Word:

_____
_____
_____

How did I apply this word today?

_____
_____
_____

Self-Evaluation: Did I miss an opportunity to apply this wisdom today?

_____
_____
_____
_____
_____
_____
_____
_____
_____
_____
_____
_____
_____
_____
_____
_____
_____
_____
_____
_____

Prejudices are a direct admission of a person's ignorance

Ignorance has always been looked upon as being a bad word, but, it's just another term for "not knowing". We are all ignorant to something but then there is what I call a "corporate ignorance". This is when a group of people adopt the same views without knowing truth or facts on a subject. God has given us all the ability to decipher right from wrong, good from evil, and the ability to judge when love is operating or when hate is operating. We should never be ignorant to what is in operation around us.

Daily Read: Acts 17:22-32

My Thoughts:

My Goal Today to Apply This Word:

How did I apply this word today?

Self-Evaluation: Did I miss an opportunity to apply this wisdom today?

_____
_____
_____
_____
_____
_____
_____
_____
_____
_____
_____
_____
_____
_____
_____
_____
_____
_____
_____
_____
_____

Private prejudice is the #1 public Enemy!

In light of the events that have taken place in the last few years regarding people's civil rights being violated, I talked with Jesus about it. He said something really thought provoking. He said, "Val sleeping giants do get up". He said, "Yes laws were passed to allow equal rights to be put in place in the land, but the deliverance from the bigotry-spirit never took place". In other words, the laws of the land did its part, but the believers didn't do our part. (Cast Out Devils) So, the giant was just asleep not slain". Spiritual warfare changes atmospheres!

Daily Read: 1 Timothy 5:20-22

My Thoughts:

_____

_____

_____

My Goal Today to Apply This Word:

_____

_____

_____

How did I apply this word today?

_____

_____

_____

Self-Evaluation: Did I miss an opportunity to apply this wisdom today?

Don't allow what someone thinks or say of you, stop the processing of you

What I love about the Father is He is all about stages, levels, and processes. Every place in our lives is a place to apply kingdom principles or flesh principles (opinions of others); and whichever we decide to apply will determine our life results. Remember, both sets of principles have a process and an outcome.

Daily Read: Philippians 3:1-16(NLT)

My Thoughts:

_____
_____
_____

My Goal Today to Apply This Word:

_____
_____
_____

How did I apply this word today?

_____
_____
_____

Self-Evaluation: Did I miss an opportunity to apply this wisdom today?

_____
_____
_____
_____
_____
_____
_____
_____
_____
_____
_____
_____
_____
_____
_____
_____
_____
_____
_____
_____
_____
_____
_____

The wheels of divine JUSTICE turn ever so slowly, but they grind ever so finely

One day I was listening to a well-respected preacher of the gospel and he made a divine statement that attached itself to my spirit and I could not allow that profoundness to fall to the ground.

In society, today you see so many people killing others with words and with actions and doing it without any reservations (consciousness) it is called **Character Assassination.** People assassinate others without a second thought of the outcome. The bible says in Gen. 8:22 "While the earth remains, seedtime and harvest, cold and heat, winter and summer, and day and night shall not cease". With that truth established, remember your words are seeds. Yes, night will fall, and seasons will change, but without-a-shadow of doubt the day is coming around when every seed must bring forth a harvest. It's called the Law of Reciprocity (what goes around comes around); be sure to plant good seeds.

Daily Read: Matthew 7

My Thoughts:

_____

_____

_____

My Goal Today to Apply This Word:

_____

_____

_____

How did I apply this word today?

_____

_____

_____

Self-Evaluation: Did I miss an opportunity to apply this wisdom today?

_____
_____
_____
_____
_____
_____
_____
_____
_____
_____
_____
_____
_____
_____
_____
_____
_____
_____
_____

Divine healing is not just a cliché, but can be a residence in a person's life on a daily basis

While writing this book my body came under attack and this quote came to life. I pulled a muscle in my hip and it was difficult for me to put weight on my left leg. I simply stated the "Divine healing power of Jesus is alive in me and every muscle and nerve must line up with the word of God". After I ministered that confession over my body, ten minutes later when I went to sit down I felt a strong pull in my hip area and the pain subsided. I simply whispered thank you Jesus for your divine healing.

Daily Read: 1 Peter 2

My Thoughts:

My Goal Today to Apply This Word:

How did I apply this word today?

Self-Evaluation: Did I miss an opportunity to apply this wisdom today?

Why would a God that takes care of you in your disobedience, abandon you in your obedience?

I see so many people in the body of Christ dealing with the issue of tithes and offerings. One day I was conversing with the Holy Spirit about it and the above-statement of wisdom was engrafted upon my heart.

Daily Read: Malachi 3

My Thoughts:

_____
_____
_____

My Goal Today to Apply This Word:

_____
_____
_____

How did I apply this word today?

_____
_____
_____

Self-Evaluation: Did I miss an opportunity to apply this wisdom today?

Fragile people always look to surround themselves with strong people, but they always tend to company themselves with "loud" people who have a façade of strength

I was sitting one day talking with my mother and the Holy Spirit dropped this truth into my heart. He said you know Isaac was an obedient man but not a very strong man, thus, he clung to the son that represented what he thought strength should look like. When the one he clung to God said he hated. I said wow! Why God? He said, "because what looks like strength to man isn't always the case to God". Esau sold his birthrights for a pot of stew; yet Jacob conquered an angel and became a nation. Due to who Jacob truly was, his name was changed to whom God said he was "Israel" which still stands today.

Daily Read: Genesis 32

My Thoughts:

_____
_____
_____

My Goal Today to Apply This Word:

_____
_____
_____

How did I apply this word today?

_____
_____
_____

Self-Evaluation: Did I miss an opportunity to apply this wisdom today?

Gossip-a person given to gossiping and divulging personal information about others; wave backwards and forwards one's tongue; speak about others and reveal secrets or intimacies.

Loudness does not necessarily constitute strength, but it can be an over compensation for a weakness

What does strength really look like? How can one know if a person walks in the ability of strength? Strength is not a characteristic, strength is more of a distinctive treasure. As a society, we have defined strength as boisterous, over-the-top actions. Today we think those that are forthright, and speaks what's on their mind are persons that are strong. I think the ability to keep silent in times where you are expected to speak shows great strength. Your strength is not in many words, but the ability to stand amid outlandish situations, and not be moved to speak words into the atmosphere that have absolutely NO VALUE to your outcome.

Daily Read: Ecclesiastes 10

My Thoughts:

_____
_____
_____

My Goal Today to Apply This Word:

_____
_____
_____

How did I apply this word today?

_____
_____
_____

Self-Evaluation: Did I miss an opportunity to apply this wisdom today?

_____
_____
_____
_____
_____
_____
_____
_____
_____
_____
_____
_____
_____
_____
_____
_____
_____
_____
_____
_____
_____
_____

Our Environment Is Everything

I am thoroughly convinced our environment shapes our views, morals, decision making process and how we handle life and its pressures. When one discounts the importance of whom they surround themselves with, where they pitch their tents, and who they allow to pour into their lives they don't care about their environment. Your environment is crucial to your outcome. Environment Is Everything!

Are your ears itching for comfort or is your heart burning for truth?

I never thought I would live to see a day where deception would become the norm. You would think people would desire truth for their lives verses a troth of deception. Personally, I found when I was living according to the desires of my itching ears, it took way too much effort to keep my life in line with the lies I had formed for myself. One day I decided to come to the realization, my life was full of misnomers. What I thought to be true was absolutely false, it was truths I had formed from my itching ears. I made up in my mind "I have to rid myself of itching ears". I had to saddle up and let truth ride me to freedom. I determined regardless of how bumpy the ride may get "I HAVE TO BE FREE"!!

Daily Read: 2 Timothy 4

My Thoughts:

_____

_____

_____

My Goal Today to Apply This Word:

_____

_____

_____

How did I apply this word today?

_____

_____

_____

Self-Evaluation: Did I miss an opportunity to apply this wisdom today?

One "good" moment in a moment does not constitute LOVE!

Moments are fleeting; they are just what they say. They are "moments". Basing relationships on temporal things will never fulfill the part of you that desires permanency. We were designed by God for lasting relationships. Be determined to have lasting relationships. If you are going to be a friend, be a real friend. If you are going to marry, be married. If you are going to connect to a church, stay connected. Because honestly speaking "good" moments only make memories; true relationships are engrafted with LOVE that gives life!

Daily Read: John 15

My Thoughts:

_____
_____
_____

My Goal Today to Apply This Word:

_____
_____
_____

How did I apply this word today?

_____
_____
_____

Self-Evaluation: Did I miss an opportunity to apply this wisdom today?

Empty people fill themselves with other people lives

The attributes of God are so beautiful and satisfying that a life-time of exploring would be too little time to tap into His in-exhaustive ways He has created to fill the void of a person's life. So be in pursuit to notice all the wonderful things God has placed here in the earth for you to richly enjoy. I promise you, you will never have another empty moment.

Daily Read: Psalms 19

My Thoughts:

_____

_____

_____

My Goal Today to Apply This Word:

_____

_____

_____

How did I apply this word today?

_____

_____

_____

Self-Evaluation: Did I miss an opportunity to apply this wisdom today?

Life owes us nothing but memories and experiences; make the right decisions, "learn" from your mistakes and you will enjoy them both

Memories and experiences can be either pleasurable or painful. How you shelve (store) them determines how you relate in your life's walk. If your bad experiences aren't placed on the right shelf, every time you have that memory it can build upon a callous that will harden your heart to the degree of a glacier. Forgiveness is everything! Remember your life is a class, so at all cost pass with flying colors. Determine to "FORGIVE'!

Daily Read: Proverbs 16:1-3

My Thoughts:

My Goal Today to Apply This Word:

How did I apply this word today?

Self-Evaluation: Did I miss an opportunity to apply this wisdom today?

People that are consumed with an unhealthy lifestyle (such as addictions) are most likely unable to make rational decisions or give someone else what they need in a healthy relationship. Never deceive yourself of the obvious!

Daily Read: Psalms 38

My Thoughts:

_____

_____

_____

My Goal Today to Apply This Word:

_____

_____

_____

How did I apply this word today?

_____

_____

_____

Self-Evaluation: Did I miss an opportunity to apply this wisdom today?

The definitions for Clique - a bunch of FLESH that talks, acts, and thinks the same. (Pastor Eddie)

Some people live according to their feelings waiting for moments to be offended, to defend, or to decipher every word coming at them. I have found people that live according to these standards tend to locate the same type of people wherever they go. We should be aware of who we draw to us, because it's not always healthy or beneficial to have people around us that are just like us. As believers, we are to develop relationships where iron is sharpening iron.

Daily Read: Galatians 5

My Thoughts:

_____
_____
_____

My Goal Today to Apply This Word:

_____
_____
_____

How did I apply this word today?

_____
_____
_____

Self-Evaluation: Did I miss an opportunity to apply this wisdom today?

There is more to life than going no-where!

To exist in this earth without a plan of progression is a slap in the master artist's face. God has created each one of us with great purpose, potential, and depth, but you must dig. I find so many times, that people become discouraged with the season of digging. Digging is going deeper into His word and allowing Jesus to show you who you are, and what you have been designed to contribute to this earth. Why you have been set in the earth is as important as the air you breathe. Your desire should be to take your life beyond the norm. Remember, it doesn't take much time to get to "NO-WHERE" but it takes a life-time to travel through DESTINY!

Daily Read: Lamentations 1:9

My Thoughts:

_____

_____

_____

My Goal Today to Apply This Word:

_____

_____

_____

How did I apply this word today?

_____

_____

_____

Self-Evaluation: Did I miss an opportunity to apply this wisdom today?

Forgiveness - *allowing room for error or weakness without skewing your view of someone*

If you are teachable you are fixable

As a woman in love with the true concept of "covenant" I am always amazed at the thousands of people convinced their situations can't be fixed. Any relationship that is open to greater information than what they currently have in their knowledge base, has the opportunity to change any given situation faced.

Marriages, friendships, working relationships, parent child relationships can change if the heart is ready to receive greater revelation than what is currently embedded in their knowledge bank.

I have learned, if you are a receiver (willing to be taught) anything is fixable. I will go even further than that and say anything can be made whole if you are teachable. (The woman at the well proves this to be true.)

Daily Read: Job 6:23 - 25

My Thoughts:

_____

_____

_____

My Goal Today to Apply This Word:

_____

_____

_____

How did I apply this word today?

_____

_____

_____

Self-Evaluation: Did I miss an opportunity to apply this wisdom today?

If you cannot quite hear God, read God!

Hearing the voice of God is an awesome way to have a relationship with the Father, it's invigorating to hear Him clearly, However, there is nothing like reading God's word to gain a greater relationship with Him as well. I found reading the word of God made me have an even greater thirst for His voice. The desire to learn more about His word being engrafted upon my heart made me listen even closer to hear from Him in the cool of the day. The great thing about spending time reading the word of God is, no one can take what your heart has stamped as life!

Daily Read: James 1:21

My Thoughts:

_____
_____
_____

My Goal Today to Apply This Word:

_____
_____
_____

How did I apply this word today?

_____
_____
_____

Self-Evaluation: Did I miss an opportunity to apply this wisdom today?

A man can never know the depth of bondage he was in until his mind has been transformed into the mind of Christ

When one thinks of bondage they tend to think of things that are seen by the natural eye, things that are notable strongholds. However, the biggest bondage man has to overcome is the bondage of conformity. Conformity is always pulling on our views, our words, and our morals. The objective of conformity is to discount transformation until it has no intrinsic value to you.

Daily Read: Romans 12:1-2

My Thoughts:

_____
_____
_____

My Goal Today to Apply This Word:

_____
_____
_____

How did I apply this word today?

_____
_____
_____

Self-Evaluation: Did I miss an opportunity to apply this wisdom today?

_____
_____
_____
_____
_____
_____
_____
_____
_____
_____
_____
_____
_____
_____
_____
_____
_____
_____
_____
_____

"Don't let your spiritual arrogance block your supernatural healing"

Daily Read: 2 Kings 5:10-15

My Thoughts:

_____
_____
_____

My Goal Today to Apply This Word:

_____
_____
_____

How did I apply this word today?

_____
_____
_____

Self-Evaluation: Did I miss an opportunity to apply this wisdom today?

_____
_____
_____
_____
_____
_____
_____
_____
_____
_____
_____

Don't allow what you don't know to determine what you are willing to hear; Remember, the Father placed people in the earth that are designed to help you maneuver through some of your toughest life challenges. The only way one will fail is the moment they decide they know everything

Daily Read: 1 Samuel 11:5-7

My Thoughts:

_____
_____
_____

My Goal Today to Apply This Word:

_____
_____
_____

How did I apply this word today?

_____
_____
_____

Self-Evaluation: Did I miss an opportunity to apply this wisdom today?

_____
_____
_____
_____
_____
_____
_____
_____
_____
_____
_____
_____
_____
_____
_____
_____
_____
_____

If life's justice system had to be served on you today what would the verdict be? Heaven or Hell?

One evening we were taking our oldest grandson to meet his parents after an afternoon with him and on our way to our destination we were redirected by police to take another route. When we arrived at the meeting point to drop our grandson off we were informed the road had been closed for over five hours due to a fatal accident. To our knowledge a young man was killed riding a motorcycle. The very moment I heard the news the Holy Spirit whispered to me the above-reference statement and I thought about this question all night. What's your take on it?

Daily Read: Acts 7

My Thoughts:

_____
_____
_____

My Goal Today to Apply This Word:

_____
_____
_____

How did I apply this word today?

_____
_____
_____

Self-Evaluation: Did I miss an opportunity to apply this wisdom today?

Worldly soul-ties will produce pondering of the heart and keeps the mind wondering

One day I was talking with a young lady who was having some difficulties in her life and the subject moved from her current situation to some past relationships that were not Godly, and she stated, "she didn't want to go back that way". Immediately this saying stamped in my spirit.

Daily Read: Proverbs 4:25-27

My Thoughts:

_____
_____
_____

My Goal Today to Apply This Word:

_____
_____
_____

How did I apply this word today?

_____
_____
_____

Self-Evaluation: Did I miss an opportunity to apply this wisdom today?

_____
_____
_____
_____
_____
_____
_____
_____
_____
_____
_____
_____
_____
_____
_____
_____
_____
_____
_____
_____
_____

Attention Seekers Are Spiritual Drainers

As a Pastor, it is a part of our job description to lend an ear to those who may need guidance along this road called life. However, it is not limited to pastors lending their ears to those in need, it is a privilege for anyone involved in meaningful relationships to open their hearts to those who need a listening ear. I have found it very rewarding to see people conqueror and win over situations and circumstances that were so easily besetting them.

Then there are those for some reason or another who have decided "I would prefer you give me the attention instead of an answer". We all have these types of individuals in our lives. They talk with us year after year about the same situation and reject any sound advice regarding a solution. I call them "Spiritual Drainers". So, I decided years ago, if I become so drained from dealing with one person, how can I be of any true service to others that desperately need and want "Change"?

Daily Read: Deuteronomy 1:42-45

My Thoughts:

_____

_____

_____

My Goal Today to Apply This Word:

_____

_____

_____

How did I apply this word today?

_____

_____

_____

Self-Evaluation: Did I miss an opportunity to apply this wisdom today?

A person standing in the middle of a drought is a person void of truth

First, we must establish in our heart that poverty of any kind; money, love, faith, temperance, sharing, etc… is death. We have to know without a shadow of doubt death has been abolished by the life Christ.

Second, we must understand it takes an investment on our part to ensure this very truth is established in our hearts (that poverty has been abolished). We cannot be persuaded by what it looks like today. We cannot allow the dictates of how we feel to move us off of the fact, poverty has been abolished. Honestly, without establishing this truth to govern our lives, drought will always be the result.

Daily Read: Isaiah 58:10-12

My Thoughts:

_____
_____
_____

My Goal Today to Apply This Word:

_____
_____
_____

How did I apply this word today?

_____
_____
_____

Self-Evaluation: Did I miss an opportunity to apply this wisdom today?

Maturity - based on slow careful consideration having completed natural growth and development: ripe, having undergone maturation: having attained a final or desired state

A current circumstance doesn't constitute a permanent decision

There are things in my life I am not very proud of, and if we would all be truthful all of us could probably make that same statement. When I accepted the call of evangelist, Holy Spirit told me, my mouth would be a trumpet to bring light and truth. In my first book, I exposed the ugly truth about women abusing children(sexually) and how I was molested by two women at two different times; but there are other truths the church must deal with so that we "will not" have spots or wrinkles. The above statement was birthed out of my reading a book called *"Divine Revelation of Heaven – by Mary Kaye Baxter"* the section on Aborted babies. One day I found myself faced with a circumstance through promiscuity (in a rebellious state of living) that forced me to choose life or death. I allowed a circumstance to cloud my view of life and what it represents (purpose, possibilities, adventures, and fulfillment), and I chose death which represents a permanent decision.

Yes, I asked God for forgiveness and I truly repented for the act of murder, and yes, I understand I must stand at judgment and give an account for that action, but thanks be to God for Jesus who paid it all and I trust the blood of Jesus and its power to cover my sins.

My friend if you have ever been faced with this decision and you chose death and you have never truly repented for your decision; today is your day to release guilt and grab hold of your righteousness in Christ Jesus.

Repeat this simple prayer: Father I ask for forgiveness and I repent for the act of murder. I renounce the murdering spirit in my bloodline and I set forth through my confession the Life cycle down to a thousand generations. Father I will use my experience to help someone else choose life. In Jesus Name Amen!

Daily Read: Revelations 9:13-21

My Thoughts:

_____
_____
_____

My Goal Today to Apply This Word:

_____
_____
_____

How did I apply this word today?

_____
_____
_____

Self-Evaluation: Did I miss an opportunity to apply this wisdom today?

_____
_____
_____
_____
_____
_____
_____
_____

When a man lives according to his references (what he knows) he is a man that walks by SIGHT! A man that lives by his confessions is a man that walks by FAITH!

Daily Read: 2 Corinthians 5

My Thoughts:

My Goal Today to Apply This Word:

How did I apply this word today?

Self-Evaluation: Did I miss an opportunity to apply this wisdom today?

The resident of a vain person is "Senseless" conversation

A vain person always thinks it's about them. Don't get me wrong you should be confident in the person you were designed to be, but it's over the top when you make it all about yourself. Yes, everyone desires to look good, dress good, and feel good about themselves. However, that is not the sum total of who you are. People often define themselves by the outer exterior and fail to develop their inner self. When we concentrate on the outer and leave the inner empty, then what proceeds out of your mouth will tell the true story of who you are.

Daily Read: Colossians 2:17-19

My Thoughts:

_____

_____

_____

My Goal Today to Apply This Word:

_____

_____

_____

How did I apply this word today?

_____

_____

_____

Self-Evaluation: Did I miss an opportunity to apply this wisdom today?

_____
_____
_____
_____
_____
_____
_____
_____
_____
_____
_____
_____
_____
_____
_____
_____
_____
_____
_____
_____
_____

A person void of substance (the Word) is the breeding ground for a busy body

As a writer, I get a lot of my inspiration from everyday life things that inspire me. There is a book in the bible that is a letter in which I love. This letter is from Paul who is writing his second letter to the church at Thessalonica. He warns them against "Idleness" being in their midst.

II Thessalonians 3:1-11. Paul states, he prays the word of the Lord runs swiftly and be glorified (manifested). Then he goes on to say he prays the Lord directs the heart of the people into Love, and finally, he states that an example of walking orderly had been among them and those that walk disorderly (or not according to the word of God) are "busybodies". To make it simple and short; get the word, get substance; a lack of the word, a lack of substance, which will result in being a busybody. This is one of my favorite reads.

Daily Read: 2 Thessalonians 3

My Thoughts:

___

My Goal Today to Apply This Word:

___

How did I apply this word today?

___

Self-Evaluation: Did I miss an opportunity to apply this wisdom today?

_____
_____
_____
_____
_____
_____
_____
_____
_____
_____
_____
_____
_____
_____
_____
_____
_____
_____
_____
_____

Our environment is a representation of our wisdom

I've looked at so many people in all different environments and the only difference I see in a prosperous man and a man lacking prosperity; is one thing, a lack of wisdom. Some people have grasped the true understanding of prosperity. There are others that find it hard to understand true wealth due to them not having a full working knowledge of inner wealth. When people hear the word wealth, they hear "money", but when I hear wealth, I hear "full-life" living from the inside out. Why some people neglect or reject the wisdom of being prosperous, I don't know. However, those that embrace the prosperity message live beyond their wildest dreams. My questions for you today is "What does your inner picture of wealth look like"? "What does your wealth environment look like"? Are you around prosperity builders or dream killers? Believe it or not, it will determine your next level.

Daily Read: Galatians 6:14-16 (Message Bible)

My Thoughts:

_____

_____

_____

My Goal Today to Apply This Word:

_____

_____

_____

How did I apply this word today?

_____

_____

_____

Self-Evaluation: Did I miss an opportunity to apply this wisdom today?

Those who are afraid to see the light (truth) wear blinders

I was talking with my husband one day about the spirit of deception and how I saw it as a spirit that really digs into the soul of man; so when the obvious is before them because of deception the obvious cannot be seen. My husband and I are pastors, so we have the awesome privilege of counseling people from all walks of life, with all types of life situations. Most of the time the obvious will be sitting right in a person's face. Nonetheless, because deception has rooted itself in them (from not facing other issues in their life) they cannot see the obvious in their current situation.

I call this type of deception "layered lies" or "comfortable lies". These are lies that have resulted from total life deception. Why? Because at some point in life the person became afraid to take the blinders off and deal with the "truth". So, the obvious then becomes the lie and deception becomes their "TRUTH". For example: A battered woman will say year after year "he only hits me because he loves me, I should not have done this when I know what he likes, he is under stress, etc…".

No, the truth is the abuser has no self-control, so they try to control others by their actions of physical or mental abuse." When a (wo)man lives in deception it's very hard to distinguish things that should be plain and clear. I see so many people walking around with blinders on, and the truth is yelling so loud even a child can hear it. ***Proverbs 1:20-21 (20) Wisdom calls aloud outside; she raises her voice in the open squares. (21) She cries out in the chief concourses; at the openings of the gates in the city she speaks her words. (22) How long you simple ones, will you love simplicity?***

Daily Read: John 8:32

My Thoughts:

_____

_____

_____

My Goal Today to Apply This Word:

_____

_____

_____

How did I apply this word today?

_____

_____

_____

Self-Evaluation: Did I miss an opportunity to apply this wisdom today?

_____

_____

_____

_____

_____

_____

_____

_____

_____

_____

_____

_____

_____

_____

_____

Every choice you make has a price tag on it!

Daily Read: Deuteronomy 30:15

My Thoughts:

_____
_____
_____

My Goal Today to Apply This Word:

_____
_____
_____

How did I apply this word today?

_____
_____
_____

Self-Evaluation: Did I miss an opportunity to apply this wisdom today?

_____
_____
_____
_____
_____
_____
_____

Your choices represent your beliefs!

Many people choose things without a thought of how their decisions reflect their belief-system. We should always ask ourselves a few questions before signing off on something.
1. "Is this truly what I believe I should do?"
2. "Is this reflective of what my core-values are?"
3. "Do I really want to be associated with this decision?"
4. "Is this what Jesus would do?"

One thing for sure your choices constitute your signature of belief. What are you signing off on?

Daily Read: 2 Thessalonians 2:12-14

My Thoughts:

_____
_____
_____

My Goal Today to Apply This Word:

_____
_____
_____

How did I apply this word today?

_____
_____
_____

Self-Evaluation: Did I miss an opportunity to apply this wisdom today?

_____
_____
_____
_____
_____
_____
_____
_____
_____
_____
_____
_____
_____
_____
_____
_____
_____
_____
_____
_____

Faith is a conscious effort…Fear takes no effort at all!

You have to put forth an effort to believe God's word, because fear (False. Evidence. Appearing. Real) is always looking for a place to reside. The bible tells us God has not given us the spirit of fear, but power, love, and sound mind. Meaning, it takes a soundness not to panic when the pressures of life are pressing up against you. It takes love operating in our life in full capacity for our faith to even work in any situation. It takes the power (tenacity) to pull on the word when your senses are showing you something different.

Fear will stand in your face and say, "Everything before you is evidence this will not work", or "What you are believing for is just not going to happen".

At that point you have to consciously make the effort to WALK BY FAITH!

Daily Read: 2 Timothy 1:7

My Thoughts:

_____

_____

_____

My Goal Today to Apply This Word:

_____

_____

_____

How did I apply this word today?

_____

_____

_____

Self-Evaluation: Did I miss an opportunity to apply this wisdom today?

Quality moments far outweigh quantifying moments

"Quality" moments are considered to be a valuable commodity filled with life-long attachments. "Quantifying" moments are designed to make one feel a sense of instant satisfaction.

My question is, which one has the greater value? "Moments" filled with quality or "Hours" void of substance? We should never want moments in our lives filled with non-valuable, non-productive things. So, which one do you choose? Quality vs. Quantity

Daily Read: Songs of Solomon 4

My Thoughts:

_____
_____
_____

My Goal Today to Apply This Word:

_____
_____
_____

How did I apply this word today?

_____
_____
_____

Self-Evaluation: Did I miss an opportunity to apply this wisdom today?

What if some were unfaithful? Will their unfaithfulness nullify God's faithfulness?

Romans 3:3

Justification is only needed when a "LIE" is covering the truth

When I was given this revelation, I even questioned it myself. I said if someone is telling the truth there is no need for justification. Then the Holy Spirit with all His wisdom ministered to me "if someone has to justify the truth then that means someone has told a lie to contradict the truth being told". Wow!

Daily Read: Roman 3:3-4

My Thoughts:

_____

_____

_____

My Goal Today to Apply This Word:

_____

_____

_____

How did I apply this word today?

_____

_____

_____

Self-Evaluation: Did I miss an opportunity to apply this wisdom today?

Eternity Is A Destination Are You Ready For It?

I know it has been said we are living eternity right now and I can agree; however, I am referencing when you put down mortality and pick up immortality. For the most part man is not accustomed to thinking about finality until they are faced with the reality their life here in the earth realm is coming to a close. Eternity should be at the forefront of our minds daily. This brief time, "in time", gives us experiences and opportunities to pave the way for our eternal life. We should live our lives as if we are navigating through a maze looking for the expected end.

Daily Read: 2 Peter 2

My Thoughts:

_____
_____
_____

My Goal Today to Apply This Word:

_____
_____
_____

How did I apply this word today?

_____
_____
_____

Self-Evaluation: Did I miss an opportunity to apply this wisdom today?

When you find a man that thinks he knows everything; that's a man you cannot teach anything.
(Pastor Eddie)

Daily Read: Proverbs 17

My Thoughts:

_____

_____

_____

My Goal Today to Apply This Word:

_____

_____

_____

How did I apply this word today?

_____

_____

_____

Self-Evaluation: Did I miss an opportunity to apply this wisdom today?

_____

_____

_____

_____

_____

_____

_____

When one lives for tomorrow he can miss the greatest opportunities of today. Stay focused and don't get lost day-dreaming!

Day-dreaming about how it could be, takes time away from seizing the moments of today. Today, your business partner could be right in front of you; your dream job could be awaiting your arrival. That relationship that will change your life forever could be staring you right in the face. Great opportunities are awaiting you today, but if you make excuses for why you can't seize the moment, you'll get lost waiting for the perfect moment!

Daily Read: Proverbs 8:11-13

My Thoughts:

_____

_____

_____

My Goal Today to Apply This Word:

_____

_____

_____

How did I apply this word today?

_____

_____

_____

Self-Evaluation: Did I miss an opportunity to apply this wisdom today?

If the word of God isn't given to you plain & straight, count on having a life "crooked & crazy"

Daily Read: Proverbs 8:11-13

My Thoughts:

_____
_____
_____

My Goal Today to Apply This Word:

_____
_____
_____

How did I apply this word today?

_____
_____
_____

Self-Evaluation: Did I miss an opportunity to apply this wisdom today?

_____
_____
_____
_____
_____
_____
_____

When you wish you had what another man has, you lessen what God has done for you!

I always find it amazing when people can't celebrate what God is doing in someone else's life. It's like we limit God to what we currently have. What you have now it's not all that God possesses. His resources are so unlimited, even if you had a hundred-lifetimes you would not be able to tap into the abundance of God.

Never reduce God down to where you are, or think he can't handle your tomorrow. In reality we could never keep up with God or his vastness.

He's Amazing!

Daily Read: Psalms 68:15-17

My Thoughts:

_____
_____
_____

My Goal Today to Apply This Word:

_____
_____
_____

How did I apply this word today?

_____
_____
_____

Self-Evaluation: Did I miss an opportunity to apply this wisdom today?

Whatever occupies your mind, masters your life!

If we took care of our thought life the way we take care of our outer appearance, there would be more fruitful results in our lives and lot less unfruitful days. The bible tells us plainly to think on things that are pure, lovely, and good report. Why? Because virtue (strength) resides in all those things.

Daily Read: Philippians 4:7-9

My Thoughts:

_____

_____

_____

My Goal Today to Apply This Word:

_____

_____

_____

How did I apply this word today?

_____

_____

_____

Self-Evaluation: Did I miss an opportunity to apply this wisdom today?

He knew about "this" day on yesterday, that is why on "that" day He did not tell you about today; because if he did you would not have walked it out by faith

Sometimes when the pressures of life are presented to us, we want God to remove the pressure and give immediate relief. Immediate relief does not produce faith, it produces fainters.

Daily Read:
2 Corinthians 5:6-8 & Psalms 27:13-14

My Thoughts:

_____
_____
_____

My Goal Today to Apply This Word:

_____
_____
_____

How did I apply this word today?

_____
_____
_____

Self-Evaluation: Did I miss an opportunity to apply this wisdom today?

True living is when you stop pretending something is dead when it is still alive

Facing a traumatic life issue (mind traumas), which we desire to be dead can be the hardest task of one's life. Why? Because things that run so deep in our soul (mind, will, emotions and intellect) can literally tear a life apart if we don't deal with it properly. I have found, pretending something doesn't exist gives a person the "freedom" (artificial relief) to live a life from under the pressure of what they know to be true. However, we are called to live a life of truth, freedom, and abundance. If you really want to bury something, remove the lie from it, then face it, dispel every untruth attached to it, then you relinquish its power over you. Truth is designed to put every lie, every habit, every mind trauma, and fear to death. Truth is the giver of life. Whom the Son has made free is free indeed!

Daily Read: John 4:14 -24

My Thoughts:

_____
_____
_____

My Goal Today to Apply This Word:

_____
_____
_____

How did I apply this word today?

_____
_____
_____

Self-Evaluation: Did I miss an opportunity to apply this wisdom today?

A man that wants the glory without the story will never be able to see the kingdom of God

We must understand God will justify (purge) us before He glorifies us. Without the word of God being tested in our lives there is no place for the glory of God to reside in our life. Process is the best friend to a believer.

Daily Read: Deuteronomy 8:1-3

My Thoughts:

_____
_____
_____

My Goal Today To Apply This Word

_____
_____
_____

How did I apply this word today?

_____
_____
_____

Self-Evaluation: Did I miss an opportunity to apply this wisdom today?

_____
_____
_____
_____
_____
_____
_____
_____
_____
_____
_____
_____
_____
_____
_____
_____
_____
_____
_____

Your time is never wasted when it makes two people the best of friends

Friendship is like a marriage it must be developed, cultivated, and groomed. Don't just walk away from an ordained friendship because of disagreements, difference of opinions, or because you may see flaws in the other person. You were ordained for your friend. You have been placed in that person's life to show forth the love of Christ and uniqueness of friendship like Christ did with the disciples.

Question: Can you look beyond the fault and see the need?

Daily Read: Job 29:1-4

My Thoughts:

_____

_____

_____

My Goal Today to Apply This Word:

_____

_____

_____

How did I apply this word today?

_____

_____

_____

Self-Evaluation: Did I miss an opportunity to apply this wisdom today?

_____
_____
_____
_____
_____
_____
_____
_____
_____
_____
_____
_____
_____
_____
_____
_____
_____
_____
_____
_____

Don't allow what "you know" to determine what you are willing to hear (receive). Remember, the Father places people in the earth that are designed to help you maneuver through some of your toughest life challenges.

Daily Read: Mark 4:1-9

My Thoughts:

_____

_____

_____

My Goal Today to Apply This Word:

_____

_____

_____

How did I apply this word today?

_____

_____

_____

Self-Evaluation: Did I miss an opportunity to apply this wisdom today?

The only way someone will ever fail is the moment they decide they have reached their capacity to download. We are ever "Learning"

Daily Read:
Prov. 11:3 NIV

My Thoughts:
_____
_____
_____

My Goal Today to Apply This Word:
_____
_____
_____

How did I apply this word today?
_____
_____
_____

Self-Evaluation: Did I miss an opportunity to apply this wisdom today?
_____
_____
_____
_____
_____
_____
_____
_____
_____
_____
_____

If your self-worth is wrapped up in another man's opinion of you...you really should start unwrapping

Daily Read: Matthew 16:13-15

My Thoughts:

My Goal Today to Apply This Word:

How did I apply this word today?

Self-Evaluation: Did I miss an opportunity to apply this wisdom today?

Why would you trust the enemy with your most prize possession, your words?

Daily Read: Proverbs 10:19

My Thoughts:

_____
_____
_____

My Goal Today to Apply This Word:

_____
_____
_____

How did I apply this word today?

_____
_____
_____

Self-Evaluation: Did I miss an opportunity to apply this wisdom today?

Be true to integrity at all times, the camera is always on, and there are people watching your life

Paul writes to the church at Ephesus telling them the importance of being light or having integrity in dark places. Paul tells us that we no longer have to live in darkness because the light of Jesus has been shed abroad in our hearts. Our integrity is an indicator that we have the light of Christ guiding our moral compass.

Daily Read: Hebrews 12:1

My Thoughts:

_____
_____
_____

My Goal Today to Apply This Word:

_____
_____
_____

How did I apply this word today?

_____
_____
_____

Self-Evaluation: Did I miss an opportunity to apply this wisdom today?

A person that talks too much could have something to hide

The greatest asset God has given each of us is the ability to listen. I think we as humans don't put enough value on the art of talking less. Much can be learned in those moments of allowing others to speak. Never think "not" being heard is someone lessening your intelligence. Actually, the most intelligent person in a room is the one who gathers all the information shared and then put it to great use in their own lives.

Daily Read: James 1:18-20

My Thoughts:

_____
_____
_____

My Goal Today to Apply This Word:

_____
_____
_____

How did I apply this word today?

_____
_____
_____

Self-Evaluation: Did I miss an opportunity to apply this wisdom today?

Learn to be comfortable with yourself; then others will not have a problem with being comfortable with you

Never try to live up to someone else's "big idea" of you. Know who you are, be comfortable in who you are, live with only the expectation you place on yourself, and "NEVER" live to please the idea of what someone else may have conjured up of you.

#AuthenticityIsPriceless

Daily Read: Genesis 1:26-28

My Thoughts:

_____

_____

_____

My Goal Today to Apply This Word:

_____

_____

_____

How did I apply this word today?

_____

_____

_____

Self-Evaluation: Did I miss an opportunity to apply this wisdom today?

_____
_____
_____
_____
_____
_____
_____
_____
_____
_____
_____
_____
_____
_____
_____
_____
_____
_____
_____
_____

Being intelligent doesn't mean you are a person with wisdom!

Intellect can only relate to natural things. Intellect can only analyze what can be seen. Intellect has a limit to how far it can go. However, wisdom is limitless. Wisdom only operates in the faith realm. It is the result of you tapping into the heart of God and extracting His perfect plan for your life. Wisdom is the principal thing!

Daily Read: Proverbs 4

My Thoughts:

_____
_____
_____

My Goal Today to Apply This Word:

_____
_____
_____

How did I apply this word today?

_____
_____
_____

Self-Evaluation: Did I miss an opportunity to apply this wisdom today?

A foolish (wo)man will always heed to the counsel of the imprudent!

Have you ever met someone in passing and you happen to dive into a conversation with them and their philosophy on life, religion, relationships, money matters etc… are totally irrational? Within the conversation you happen to find out they know someone you know, and you know for a fact the person that you both know operates their life outside of the realm wisdom. "And the light bulb comes on", ahhh, so this is why you think this way. Birds of a feather flock together.

Daily Read: Proverbs 26: 1-9

My Thoughts:

_____

_____

_____

My Goal Today To Apply This Word

_____

_____

_____

How did I apply this word today?

_____

_____

_____

Self-Evaluation: Did I miss an opportunity to apply this wisdom today?

Chosen To Change The Atmosphere

You have been given the mandate to be the difference you want to see. Remember when you were formed God said...

"Then God said, "Let us make human beings in our image, to be like us. They will reign over the fish in the sea, the birds in the sky, the livestock, all the wild animals on the earth, and the small animals that scurry along the ground."

So God created human beings in his own image.
   In the image of God he created them;
   male and female he created them.

Then God blessed them and said, "Be fruitful and multiply. Fill the earth and govern it.

Have you had your spiritual "bone density" test lately? It is quick and simple: Is there Envy in your heart? Envy is rottenness to the bone.

Daily Read: Proverbs 8:11-13

My Thoughts:

_____
_____
_____

My Goal Today to Apply This Word:

_____
_____
_____

How did I apply this word today?

_____
_____
_____

Self-Evaluation: Did I miss an opportunity to apply this wisdom today?

Don't live your life today in such a way; that others would not want to help you tomorrow!

Being kind doesn't take being a rocket scientist. Being kind doesn't cost money. Being kind doesn't require higher education. Being kind doesn't cause sleep deprivation. We should always live our lives in a way that if we need help on tomorrow our yesterday hasn't diminished any life-lines.

Daily Read: Luke 10:25-37

My Thoughts:

_____
_____
_____

My Goal Today to Apply This Word:

_____
_____
_____

How did I apply this word today?

_____
_____
_____

Self-Evaluation: Did I miss an opportunity to apply this wisdom today?

Never make a man or his things your god; because he could wake up one morning and decide you are not worthy of his company.

Daily Read: Proverbs 23: 1-7

My Thoughts:
_____
_____
_____

My Goal Today to Apply This Word:
_____
_____
_____

How did I apply this word today?
_____
_____
_____

Self-Evaluation: Did I miss an opportunity to apply this wisdom today?

Love is the depth of a man's soul that cannot be measured by mere actions, attitude or association; Love is the inner part that only the creator knows, and is able to develop

Allowing God to develop love in you goes far beyond some mere feelings. It goes beyond your limited intellect. It goes beyond your human ability. It goes beyond anything you can do by mere actions. When God develops His love "Agape" in you, you begin to live a life that is beyond anything you can express that will make another person understand the magnitude that resides in your human heart. THE GOD KIND OF LOVE IS UNEXPLAINABLE!

Daily Read: 1 John 4:18

My Thoughts:

_____

_____

My Goal Today To Apply This Word

_____

_____

How did I apply this word today?

_____

_____

Self-Evaluation: Did I miss an opportunity to apply this wisdom today?

People may think they are getting by, but just know they are not getting away! (Mudear - Willie Belle Dunnigan)

Nothing that is done on earth is a surprise to God. He isn't overwhelmed by sin, sickness, disasters, death, poverty, arrogance, politics or our unbelief. ***Psalms 2:1-4 Why do the nations conspire and the peoples plot in vain? [2] The kings of the earth rise up and the rulers band together against the LORD and against his anointed, saying,[3] "Let us break their chains and throw off their shackles." [4] The One enthroned in heaven laughs; the Lord scoffs at them.*** He is fully aware of everything, everyone, and every assignment that came or has come to discourage you. Nothing, not-one-single thing isn't known by Him about you. Relax, you are Covered!

Daily Read: Ecclesiastes 1:9-14

My Thoughts:

_____
_____
_____

My Goal Today to Apply This Word:

_____
_____
_____

How did I apply this word today?

_____
_____
_____

Self-Evaluation: Did I miss an opportunity to apply this wisdom today?

Your wits may get you a promotion, but can your character keep you promoted?

Daily Read: Proverbs 20: 5-8(NLT)

My Thoughts:

_____
_____
_____

My Goal Today to Apply This Word:

_____
_____
_____

How did I apply this word today?

_____
_____
_____

Self-Evaluation: Did I miss an opportunity to apply this wisdom today?

Don't ever allow your spirit-man to be so depleted, that you have to declare spiritual bankruptcy

Spiritual dryness or depletion doesn't just affect our spiritual countenance, but it also affects us mentally, and emotionally. Sometimes as believers we can pretend as though we are engaged in our spiritual development, when the truth is, we are feeling depleted. The first mistake a person makes dealing with spiritual dryness, or feeling hard-pressed about being in the presence of God, is not admitting "I am struggling" or "I am feeling dryness in my walk with Christ". I have found people tend to think that if I admit spiritual dryness they will be looked upon as not having faith. Those negative self-inflicted thoughts are there to drive one farther away from their relationship with Christ. The second mistake is not having an accountability partner. It is spiritually healthy to have others on this journey with you. We have to stop the "long ranger" mentality in the body of Christ, even Jesus had 12-friends.

How does one get out of a spiritual dry slump? The first thing one must do is find another way of approaching their relationship with Jesus Christ. Your daily approach to your relationship on a has to change. For instance, change the type of praise and worship songs you listen to, change the time you pray, change the version of the bible you read, change the place you pray, etc… . I promise you, approach the throne differently and you will get a different response.

Daily Read: Isaiah 40:28-31

My Thoughts:

_____
_____
_____

My Goal Today To Apply This Word

_____
_____
_____

How did I apply this word today?

_____
_____
_____

Self-Evaluation: Did I miss an opportunity to apply this wisdom today?

_____
_____
_____
_____
_____
_____
_____
_____
_____
_____
_____
_____
_____
_____

When one lives for tomorrow he can miss the greatest opportunities of today. Stay focus and don't get lost day-dreaming!

Daily Read: Philippians 4:8-9

My Thoughts:

_____

_____

_____

My Goal Today to Apply This Word:

_____

_____

_____

How did I apply this word today?

_____

_____

_____

Self-Evaluation: Did I miss an opportunity to apply this wisdom today?

_____

_____

_____

_____

_____

Self-Evaluation: Did I miss an opportunity to apply this wisdom today?

Everything alive ain't always living.
(Mudear - Willie Belle Dunnigan)

This saying is dedicated to my grandmother, a woman that was full of wisdom. I think this generation has lost the art of appreciating the wisdom of our elder statesmen. As I grew in my knowledge of God and the kingdom of God (Gods way of doing things) I began to see this statement unfold right before my eyes. Daily I see people breaking their necks to make more money, become more popular, outsmart the next man, and the list goes on and on. However, a lot of those same people are not enjoying the abundant life God promised we could have. To see people, place a price tag on their journey through life, and miss the real reason for their trip to earth saddens my heart. True living looks like this: peace, joy, fulfillment, and love. Those things will never have a price attached to them. Being alive and living are two different things, no the difference. Selah

Daily Read: John 10:10

My Thoughts:

_____

_____

_____

My Goal Today to Apply This Word:

_____

_____

_____

How did I apply this word today?

_____

_____

_____

Self-Evaluation: Did I miss an opportunity to apply this wisdom today?

"Don't put your goods up for rent, when there is someone truly looking to buy". (marriage vs. shacking)

No one will value you if you don't place a value on yourself. Valuing yourself is the greatest gift you can give to yourself. When God made you, He made you priceless. Not even the most precious gem known to man is worth more than you. The gift you are to this world is far beyond what you can think or imagine. Celebrate your exquisiteness and never devalue yourself because of an emotional connection to a counterfeit. When the authentic ordained person comes in your life they will want to secure their place in your life without hesitation. You Are Valuable!

Daily Read: Psalms 139: 13-15 (ERV)

My Thoughts:

_____
_____
_____

My Goal Today to Apply This Word:

_____
_____
_____

How did I apply this word today?

_____
_____
_____

Self-Evaluation: Did I miss an opportunity to apply this wisdom today?

Your living must line up with your giving; not your giving lining up with your living

One day I was accessing our (Pastor Eddie & myself) lives and we concluded, "We were living above our means". The money was there but our giving was suffering from our lifestyle. I walked in our closet and it hit me "your giving has been subjected to your living and it is stifling your life". I thought at that moment this must change TODAY! And this line of wisdom was birthed in my heart.

Daily Read: Luke 6:38

My Thoughts:

_____
_____
_____

My Goal Today to Apply This Word:

_____
_____
_____

How did I apply this word today?

_____
_____
_____

Self-Evaluation: Did I miss an opportunity to apply this wisdom today?

Some people live, learn, and then die...some people live, never learn a thing, and still die
(Mudear - Willie Belle Dunnigan)

Life is funny! Children want to be adults and adults so many times acting like children. The thing is a child does not realize mistakes that are made in ignorance are forgiven much faster. On the other hand, a mistake made "with age behind it" is a different story. Society tends to think with age comes some sense of knowledge of right and wrong, good & evil, or moral & immoral. On the contrary there are men (man-kind) with the age of an adult but operating their lives with the mind of a child. Paul states it the best. ***"When I was a child I thought (my actions and words were childish) but when I became a man I put away childish things.*** Think about it, children are not loyal, nor do they take to constructive criticism well, nor do they look for the proper ways to handle day-to-day conflicts. So, this truth was birthed out of me truly wanting to walk in a level of maturity and to live my life on the front end of the above-referenced statement.

Daily Read: Proverbs 24:1--6

My Thoughts:

_____

_____

_____

My Goal Today to Apply This Word:

_____

_____

_____

How did I apply this word today?

_____

_____

_____

_____

Self-Evaluation: Did I miss an opportunity to apply this wisdom today?

www.ingramcontent.com/pod-product-compliance
Lightning Source LLC
Chambersburg PA
CBHW070616300426
44113CB00010B/1552